TAO TE CHING

A new version by Sam Torode,
based on a 1919 translation by Dwight Goddard.
Copyright © 2021 Sam Torode.

Published by Ancient Renewal,
an imprint of Sam Torode Book Arts,
www.samtorode.com

WHAT IS THE TAO?

The Tao that can be understood
is not the eternal, cosmic Tao,
just as an idea that can be expressed in words
is not the infinite idea.

And yet this ineffable Tao
is the source of all spirit and matter;
expressing itself,
it is the mother of all created things.

Not to desire material things
is to know the freedom of spirituality;
and to desire them is to suffer
the limitations of matter.

Yet these two things, matter and spirit,
so different in nature, have the same origin.

This unity is the mystery of mysteries,
and the gateway to spirituality.

OPPOSITES

When beauty is only a masquerade,
it is actually ugliness.
And goodness, if it is not sincere,
is not really goodness.

Existence and nonexistence are incompatible.
The difficult and the easy are mutually opposed.
The long and the short, the high and the low,
the loud and soft, the before and the after—
all are opposites.
Each reveals the other.

The wise are not conspicuous in their actions
or given to much talking.
When troubles arise,
they are not irritated.

They produce, but do not hoard;
They act, but expect no praise;
They build, but do not dwell therein.

And because they do not dwell therein,
They never depart.

RESTRAINT

When a ruler is silent on the subject of virtue,
the people are discouraged from practicing it.
Meanwhile, a ruler who revels in riches
encourages thievery.

Value virtue over wealth,
and the people's hearts will be at rest.

Wise rulers do not accumulate treasures,
but seek to quiet the hearts of their people.
They soothe the people's appetites
and strengthen their bones.
They treasure innocence,
and protect the simple from the schemes of the clever.

When a ruler practices restraint,
everything will be in peace.

THE ETERNAL TAO

The Tao seems empty,
yet it is never exhausted.

Oh, it is profound!
It existed before anything.

It dulls its own sharpness,
breaks its own bonds,
dims its own brightness,
identifies with its own dust.

Oh, it is peaceful!
It is infinite, eternal.

No one knows from where it came.
It is older than the gods.

IMPARTIALITY

The earth and the stars do not take sides—
they are impartial.

They regard all individuals as insignificant,
as though they were playthings made of straw.

The wise are also impartial;
to them all people are equal and alike.

The space between earth and the stars is like a bellows—
it is empty but does not collapse;
as it contracts, it creates.

Gossips, by contrast, spew out words till they are empty,
because they are not impartial.

THE SOURCE

The Spirit of the perennial spring
is said to be immortal.
She is called the Mysterious One.

The Mysterious One is the source of the universe.
She is continually, endlessly giving forth life,
without effort.

HUMILITY

The universe is eternal, and earth is lasting.

The reason the universe and earth are eternal and lasting
is that they do not exist for themselves.
That is why they endure.

The wise humble themselves—
and because of their humility,
they are worthy of praise.

They put others first,
and so become great.

They are not focused on outcomes or achievements;
therefore they always succeed.

GOODNESS

True goodness is like water;
it nurtures everything and harms nothing.
Like water, it ever seeks the lowest place,
the place that all others avoid.

This is the way of the Tao.
For a dwelling it chooses the quiet meadow;
for a heart the circling eddy.

In generosity it is kind;
in speech it is sincere;
in power it is order;
in action it is gentle;
in movement it is rhythm.

Because it is always peaceable,
it soothes and refreshes.

PRUDENCE

If you continue filling a pail after it is full,
the water will be wasted.
If you continue grinding an axe after it is sharp,
the edge will wear away.

Who can protect a house full of gold and jewels?
Excessive fortune brings about its own misfortune.

To win true merit—to earn a good reputation—
you must be prudent.
This is the way of the Tao.

LEAD WITHOUT FORCE

By patience, you can discipline your desires.
By self-control, you can develop strong character.
By practicing gentleness, you can become as a little child.
By purifying the subconscious, you may become perfect.

Because wise rulers love the people,
they lead without using force.

In measuring out rewards,
wise rulers act like mother birds.
While seeing into every corner,
they are unobtrusive.
While protecting the people,
they do not control them.

They are motherly and fatherly,
but not domineering.
They persuade with words, not weapons.
This is their crowning virtue.

IMMATERIALITY

A wheel may have thirty spokes,
but its usefulness lies in the empty hub.

A jar is formed from clay,
but its usefulness lies in the empty center.

A room is made from four walls,
but its usefulness lies in the space between.

Matter is necessary to give form,
but the value of reality lies in its immateriality.

Everything that lives has a physical body,
but the value of a life is measured by the soul.

SEEK THE SPIRIT

Too much light blinds the eye;
too much noise deafens the ear;
too many spices dull the taste;
too much exercise weakens the body;
the pursuit of great riches leads to ruin.

The wise attend to the inner truth of things
and are not fooled by outward appearances.
They ignore matter and seek the spirit.

AVOID EXTREMES

Flattery and disgrace are both to be feared,
just as overeating and starvation
are both harmful to the body.

Flattery is fattening to the spirit;
disgrace is emaciating.

Over-concern is just as harmful as disregard.
Treat yourself well, but don't pamper yourself excessively.

If rulers treat the people in this same way—
neither too soft nor too hard—
they are worthy to be trusted with authority.

THE MYSTERIOUS TAO

It is unseen because it is colorless;
it is unheard because it is silent;
if you try to grasp it, it will elude you,
because it has no form.

Because of its diverse qualities it cannot be summarized,
yet it comprises an essential unity.
On the surface it appears incomprehensible,
but in the depths it reveals itself.

It has been nameless forever!
It appears and then disappears.
It is the form of the formless,
the image of the imageless.

Its face cannot be seen in front,
nor its back from behind.
No one knows where it came from,
or where it is going.

Yet, by holding fast to the ancient Tao,
the wise may grasp the present,
because they understand the past.

This is a clue to the Tao.

ANCIENT MASTERS

In ancient times, the masters were subtle,
spiritual, profound, and wise.
Their thoughts could not be easily understood.

They were cautious as men wading across a river;
they were alert as soldiers in wartime;
they were reserved as guests in another's home;
they were elusive as ice at the point of melting;
they were lowly as a valley between mountains;
they were obscure as muddy waters.

Since they were difficult to understand,
I will try to make their thoughts clear.

To clarify muddy waters,
you must hold them still and let things settle.
To glimpse the secret of the Tao,
you must keep still and quiet your mind.

KNOW ETERNITY

Seek an open mind—the ideal of vacuity.
Seek composure—the essence of tranquility.

All things are in process, rising and returning.
Plants blossom for a season, then return to the root.

In returning to the root, we find tranquility;
this leads to our destiny, which is eternity.
To know eternity is enlightenment;
to ignore eternity is to invite calamity.

Knowing eternity means seeing the big picture;
seeing the big-picture is broad-minded;
breadth of vision brings nobility;
nobility is close to divinity.

The Tao is divine.
The Tao is the Eternal.
Death is not to be feared.

INVISIBLE LEADERS

If a ruler lacks faith,
so will the people.

Unworthy rulers are despised.
Common rulers are feared by their subjects.
Good rulers win the affection and praise of their subjects.

But when great rulers lead,
the people are hardly aware of their existence.

How carefully wise rulers choose their words;
how simple are their actions.
Under such a government,
the people think they are ruling themselves.

HYPOCRISY

The great Tao is ignored,
yet we speak of goodness and righteousness.

Relatives are unfriendly,
yet we talk of familial love and respect.

The state and the family are in confusion and chaos,
yet we praise ourselves for loyalty and faithfulness.

This is great hypocrisy.

FALSE AND TRUE RELIGION

Abandon the pretense of saintliness and asceticism,
and the people will pursue virtue.

Abandon ostentatious benevolence
and conspicuous righteousness;
then the people will return to the core virtues
of love and respect.

Abandon cleverness and greed;
then thieves and robbers will disappear.

Here are the four fundamentals of true spirituality:
recognize simplicity,
cherish purity,
reduce your possessions,
diminish your desires.

COMMON PEOPLE

If you would be at peace,
beware of great knowledge.

That which is not feared by the common people
is probably not worth worrying about.

There is a vast difference between book learning
and true knowledge of the Tao!

Common people are joyful—they celebrate feast days,
and hold festivals in spring time.

Scholars scowl like babies that have not learned to smile;
they look forlorn, like homeless wanderers!

Common people have plenty;
scholars are never satisfied.

Common people are vibrant with common sense;
scholars seem dull and confused.

Common people are useful;
scholars are useless.

Knowledge of the Tao, how vast!
I am like a sailor far from shore,
adrift on a boundless ocean.

Oh, how I long to be as a child,
suckling milk from Mother Tao!

THE HEART OF THE TAO

All the many forms of virtue flow from the Tao,
but the nature of the Tao is infinitely illusive.

Illusive, indeed,
but at its heart is all being.

Unfathomable, indeed,
but at its heart is all spirit,
and spirit is reality.

At its heart is truth.

The Tao is eternal and unceasing—
it is present at all beginnings.

How do I know this?
By the same Tao.

REDEMPTION

At that time, the broken will be made perfect;
the bent will be made straight;
the empty will be filled;
the worn-out will be renewed;
those having little will obtain much;
and those having much will be overcome.

The wise, embracing unity,
will become the world's model.

Not striving, they will become enlightened;
not asserting themselves, they will become distinguished;
not boasting, they will be praised;
not building up themselves, they will endure.

As much as they embrace the world,
the world will embrace them.

Is the old saying, "The broken shall be restored,"
a false hope?

No! All will be restored
and return rejoicing.

PEACE

Peace is meant to be our natural state.

A whirlwind never outlasts the morning,
nor a violent rain the day.
Just as earth and sky return to peace,
so should we.

They who act with violence become violent.
They who act with virtue become virtuous.
They who act in the spirit of the Tao become Tao-like.

They who follow the Tao, the Tao will guide.
They who pursue virtue, virtue will reward.
They who live by violence, violence will soon destroy.

SELF-ASSERTION

It is unnatural to walk on tiptoe.
Try to elevate yourself above others,
and you will soon fall.

Those who display themselves do not shine;
those who inflate themselves do not grow;
those who assert themselves do not gain merit.

The relation of these things—
self-display, self-inflation, and self-assertion—
to the Tao is the same as fat to lean meat.

They are unhealthy excesses,
fit to be trimmed off and discarded.
The Tao is not in them.

THE MOTHER OF ALL

There is Being that encompasses all,
and it existed before earth or the universe.
Calm, indeed, and immaterial;
it is singular and changeless.

All creation flows from it and returns to it.
It is the world's mother.
I cannot define it, but I will call it Tao.

If forced to describe it, I will call it great.
The great is evasive,the evasive is distant,
the distant is ever coming near.

The Tao is great.
So is the universe great,
so is earth,
and so is humanity.

Humanity is the child of earth;
Earth is the child of the universe;
The universe is the child of the Tao.

The Tao has no mother,
but is mother of all.

SELF-MASTERY

The light overcomes the heavy;
the still overcomes the frantic.

The wise never forget their dignity;
though surrounded by dazzling sights,
they remain calm and unmoved.

How did it happen that the emperor,
master of ten thousand chariots,
lost control of his empire?

Being flippant himself,
he lost the respect of his subjects.
Failing to control himself,
he lost the control of the empire.

HIDDEN VALUES

Good hikers need no maps;
good speakers need no scripts;
good counters need no abacus;
good guards need no locks.

The wise, trusting in goodness,
see the potential in others,
treating no one as an outcast.

Trusting in goodness,
they redeem all things—
nothing is worthless to them.

They recognize hidden value.

The wise take the lost under their wings,
and so the lost become newfound treasures of the wise.

Each is valuable to the other.
This is the significance of spirituality.

KNOW YOURSELF

Those who know both their masculine
and their feminine sides
become fruitful like the valleys of earth.

Being like the valleys of earth,
their vitality will not desert them—
they will remain energetic as children.

Those who know both their strengths and their limits
become models worth following.

Being worthy models,
their vitality will not fail them
—they will radiate simplicity.

Radiating simplicity,
wise rulers inspire others to follow their path.
Such is the making of a great administration.

POWER

Those who try to seize power and remake society will fail.
Society is a divine thing that cannot be remade.
One who attempts to remake it will only deface it.

Those who grasp for power will lose it.

People differ—some lead, others follow;
some are passionate, others are reserved;
some are strong, others weak;
some succeed, others fail.

The wise respect the roles of all,
and seek moderation in all things.

FIRM BUT NOT FORCEFUL

When rulers follow the Tao,
they have no need for armies to strengthen their country;
their country is strong
because its government is a blessing to all.

Briars and thorns spring up wherever an army camps.
Great wars are followed by bad harvests.

Good rulers are firm,
but they dare not take by force.
They are firm but not boastful;
firm but not haughty;
firm but not arrogant;
firm but yielding to the unavoidable;
firm but not resorting to violence.

When rulers resort to force,
things flourish for a time, but then decay.
They are going against the Tao,
and anything opposed to the Tao will soon die.

AVOID WAR

Among all tools, weapons alone are cursed;
all men come to despise them.

Those who follow Tao do not need them.
Weapons are not the tools of the wise;
only as a last resort do the wise use them.

Peace and tranquility are valued by wise rulers.
Even when victorious in battle, they do not rejoice,
for they never exalt over the killing of others.

Those rulers who rejoice over killing others
will never bring happiness to their people.

The killing of others fills the people with sorrow.
We lament with tears because of it,
and honor the victors solemnly,
as if we were attending a funeral ceremony.

WHERE TO STOP

The eternal Tao is unnamable.
In its simplicity it appears insignificant,
but the whole world cannot contain it.

If rulers would follow it,
their citizens would pay homage.
If the people would follow it,
they would have no need of rulers.

Earth and sky are made one by it,
forming sweet dew drops.
When the Tao expresses itself in creation,
it becomes visible.

If you follow the Tao,
you will understand where to stop.
Knowing where to stop,
you will be free from danger.

The Tao is like a stream
that empties into an ocean.

IMMORTALITY

Those who know others are intelligent;
those who understand themselves are enlightened.

Those who can conquer others have force;
those who can control themselves are mighty.

Those who dare risk death have courage;
but those who death cannot destroy are immortal.

TRUE GREATNESS

The great Tao is everywhere!
It is on both the right and the left.
All things rely upon it for their existence,
and it sustains them.

It draws praise, but is not proud.
It lovingly nourishes everything,
and is not possessive.

It desires nothing, and so it is considered small.
Yet everything returns to it,
and so it should be considered great.

The wise do not appear great among others;
and so they reveal their true greatness.

SEEK THE TAO

Trifles and dainties attract the passing people,
while the Tao goes unnoticed.

When looked at, it is not much to see;
when listened for, it can scarcely be heard;
but when put into practice, it is inexhaustible.

The world will go to those who seek the Tao;
they will find contentment, peace, and rest.

PERSUASION

That which contracts was first expanded;
that which weakens was first made strong;
that which falls was first raised up;
that which scatters was first gathered up.

It is paradoxical but true—
the tender outlasts the rigid;
the gentle defeats the strong.

Persuasion is better than compulsion.
Rulers have nothing to gain through force of arms.

STOP STRIVING

The Tao does nothing,
and yet nothing remains undone.

If rulers desire to keep everything in order,
they must first order themselves.
If rulers would follow the example of Tao,
all problems would resolve themselves.

The way of the Tao is simple—
stop striving, defeat desire.
In the absence of striving, there is peace;
in the absence of desire, there is satisfaction.

TRUE VIRTUE

True virtue makes no show of virtue,
and therefore it is really virtuous.
False virtue never loses sight of itself,
and therefore it is no longer virtue.

True virtue does not assert itself,
and therefore is unpretentious.
False virtue is acting a part,
and thereby is only pretense.

When the Tao is lost, there is only virtue;
when virtue is lost, there is only generosity;
when generosity is lost, there is only justice;
when justice is lost, only tradition remains.

Tradition reduces loyalty and good faith to a shadow;
it is the beginning of disorder.
Tradition is the mere flower of the Tao—
apart from its root it withers and dies.

The truly great embody the spirit,
not just the external appearance.
They bear fruit—not just blossoms.
They do not put on a show of virtue—
they practice it.

UNITY

Only those who attain unity
become what they are meant to be.

The heavens attained unity, and became space.
Matter attained unity, and became earth.
Spirit attained unity, and became mind.
Valleys attained unity, and rivers flowed into them.

All things that attain unity have life.
And the highest is that which produces unity.
Rulers, as they attain unity,
become models of conduct for the people.

If heaven were not space, it would fall
;if earth were not solid, it would melt;
if spirit were not unified, it would vanish;
if valleys were not unified, they would dry up.

Everything, if not for life, would dissipate.
Rulers, if they overestimate themselves, will fall.

Nobles should find their roots among the commoners,
for the high is always founded upon the low.

Great rulers identify with orphans, inferiors,
and the unworthy, because they recognize their roots
in the lowest of their people.

The wise do not desire to be set aside as precious gems,
nor discarded as worthless stones.

NONEXISTENCE

The Tao seems nonexistent,
but it is the basis of existence.

The universe, the earth, and everything in it
comes from existence,
but existence comes from nonexistence.

STUDENTS

Great students, when they hear of the Tao,
earnestly practice it.
Good students, when they hear of the Tao,
sometimes follow it and sometimes lose it.
Typical students, when they hear of the Tao,
ridicule it.

Were it not easily ridiculed, it would not be the true Tao.

Those most illumined by the Tao
are often the dimmest.
Those most advanced in the Tao
are often the furthest behind.

Those best guided by Tao
are the least self-assured.

Those high in virtue resemble lowly valleys;
the innocent are more likely to be shamed;
the best craftsmen can seem inefficient;
the most generous are indistinguishable from the poor.

The greatest square has no corners;
the greatest vessel is never filled.
The greatest sound has no speech;
the greatest form has no shape.

The Tao is obscure and without name,
and yet it is precisely this Tao
that alone can fulfill and complete.

YIN AND YANG

The Tao produces unity;
unity produces duality;
duality produces trinity;
trinity produces all things.

All things contain both the negative principle (yin)
and the positive principle (yang).
The third principle, energetic vitality (chi),
makes them harmonious.

There are some things which it is a gain to lose,
and a loss to gain.

This may not be what they teach in school,
but it is the first lesson in the Tao.

STILLNESS AND SILENCE

The soft overcomes the hard;
the flexible conquers the stiff;
the ethereal penetrates the solid.

This is why there is great advantage
in stillness and silence
over movement and speaking.

But few ever obtain the advantage,
for few practice stillness and silence.

TRUE FREEDOM

Which is better, fame or integrity?
Which is more valuable, riches or good character?
Which is more dangerous, failure or success?

Overindulgence creates waste.
Hoarding invites loss.

Those who are content with what they have
are not in danger of loss.
Those who know when to stop
are free to go on.

PERFECTIONISM

Extreme perfection seems imperfect,
for it never stops perfecting.

Extreme fulfillment appears empty,
for it never stops filling.

Extreme straightness appears crooked;
extreme skill, clumsy;
extreme eloquence, stammering.

Not extreme perfection,
but purity and clarity are the targets
at which we should aim.

CONTENTMENT

When a nation follows the Tao,
its horses are harnessed to ploughs.
When a nation ignores the Tao,
its horses are girded for war.

There is no sin greater than desire.
There is no misfortune greater than discontent.
There is no calamity greater than greed.

To know the Tao is to know contentment.

EXPLORE WITHIN

Without going abroad,
you can have knowledge of the world.
Without gazing at the stars,
you can perceive the heavenly Tao.

The more you wander, the less you know.

The wise explore without traveling,
discern without seeing,
finish without striving,
and arrive at their destination
without leaving home.

CLEVERNESS

Those who study in school become clever,
while those who practice the Tao become simple.

Again and again,
students of the Tao must humble themselves,
until they reach the state of non-doing.

Then they will do nothing,
yet leave nothing undone.

In ruling a nation,
one must not use cleverness.
The clever are not fit to command.

UNIVERSALITY

Wise rulers have boundless hearts;
for in the hearts of the people, they find their own.

The wise ruler treats the good with goodness;
and treats the not-so-good with goodness, too—
for goodness is its own reward.

The wise ruler treats the faithful with good faith;
and treats the unfaithful with good faith, too—
for good faith is its own reward.

Wise rulers are universal—
the people are their eyes and ears.

INVULNERABLE

Life is a going forth;
death is a returning home.

Out of ten people,
three are seeking life,
three are seeking death,
three are dying.
Only one is immortal.

The wise, when they travel,
are never attacked by wild beasts;
and when coming among soldiers,
they do not fear for their lives.

The rhinoceros cannot find a place to horn them,
nor the tiger a place to claw them,
nor soldiers a place to wound them.

Why?
Because the wise are invulnerable.

PROFOUND VIRTUE

The Tao gives life to all things;
virtue feeds them;
matter shapes them;
energy completes them.

This is why all things honor the Tao and esteem virtue.
Honor for the Tao and esteem for virtue
arise spontaneously.

For the Tao gives life to all creatures;
and virtue nurses them, raises them,
nurtures, matures, and protects them.

The Tao gives life freely,
making no claim of ownership.
Virtue forms them but does not force them,
raises them but does not rule them.

This is why virtue is profound.

THE TAO'S LIGHT

When creation began,
the Tao became the world's mother.

When you know your mother,
you also know that you are her child.
When you recognize that you are a child,
you will stay close to your mother
so she can keep you safe.

Those who watch their mouths and guard their actions
will be free from trouble to the end of life.
Those who babble and meddle in other's business
cannot escape from trouble, even to the end of life.

To recognize your insignificance is empowering.
To show sympathy is strength.
Those who follow the Tao's light
arrive at enlightenment.

THE PLAIN WAY

Even if you lack great learning,
still you can walk in the ways of the great Tao.
It is not ignorance, but cleverness that you should fear.

The great Way is very plain,
so the proud prefer the bypaths.

When the palace is splendid,
the fields are likely to be weedy
and the granaries empty.

To wear jewels and silks,
to flash your weapons,
to eat and drink excessively,
to store up wealth and treasure—
this is the way of robbers.

Pomp is contrary to the Tao.

A MODEL FOR OTHERS

A tree that is well-planted is not easily uprooted.
A treasure that is well-guarded is not easily taken away.
If you pass on the Tao to your children,
your family's virtue will endure.

The one who practices the Tao
shows that virtue is real.
The family that practices the Tao
shows that virtue is abiding.
The township that practices the Tao
shows that virtue is enduring.
The nation that practices the Tao
shows that virtue is expansive.
The empire that practices the Tao
shows that virtue is universal.

One person becomes a model for others,
one family for other families,
one town for other towns,
one nation for other nations,
one empire for all empires.

BECOME CHILDLIKE

The virtuous are like innocent children—
poisonous insects will not sting them,
wild beasts will not seize them,
birds of prey will not attack them.

Their bones may be weak,
and their muscles tender,
but their grasp is sure.

They know nothing of power,
yet they are bursting with life.

Their spirits are strong, indeed!
They can sob and cry all day without becoming hoarse;
their voices are harmonious, indeed!

To know this harmony is to know the eternal.
To know the eternal is to know enlightenment.
To increase life is to know blessedness.
To increase inner vitality is to gain strength.

As creatures grow and mature,
they begin to decay.
This is the opposite of the Tao—
the Tao remains ever young.

EMBRACE MYSTERY

Those who talk do not know;
those who know do not talk.

The wise shut their mouths
and watch their actions.

They dull their sharpness,
unravel their tangles,
dim their brilliance,
and embrace the mysterious.

They cannot be moved by praise or blame;
they cannot be changed by profit or loss;
they cannot be honored or humiliated.

And so the wise are truly honored.

GOOD GOVERNMENT

The government is best administered with virtue;
the army is best directed with strategy;
the people are best ruled by giving them freedom.

How do I know this is so?
By the Tao.

The more restrictions are enacted,
the poorer the people become.
The more soldiers patrol the streets,
the more disorderly the city becomes.

The more officials are crafty and cunning,
the harder the people are to control.
The more laws and orders are issued,
the more thieves and robbers abound.

The wise ruler says:
If I practice restraint,
the people will reform themselves.
If I love peace,
the people will become peaceful.
If I am not greedy,
the people will become prosperous.
If I practice simplicity,
the people will remain simple.

SIMPLE AND SQUARE

When an administration practices simplicity,
the people are content.
When an administration is nosy,
the people become unruly.

When the labor of the many
supports the happiness of the few,
such "happiness" only conceals misery.

Who can stop the cycle? It never ceases.
The normal becomes abnormal.
The fortunate becomes unfortunate.
The people are kept in confusion.

Wise rulers are square, but they do not poke;
they are angular, but do not injure;
they are upright, but not cross;
they are bright, but not glaring.

LIFE WITHOUT LIMITS

In ruling and in life,
nothing surpasses moderation.

One must form the habit early.
Acquiring moderation results in accumulating virtue.
By accumulating virtue, nothing is impossible.

If nothing is impossible, one knows no limits.
If one knows no limits, one may rule the empire.

Those who possess moderation will endure;
they have deep roots and strong stems.

This is the secret to a long life,
and lasting insight into the Tao.

FEARLESS

One should do great things as one fries small fish—
simply, boldly, without fear.

By following the Tao,
one may successfully rule an empire.
Ghosts will not frighten,
gods will not harm,
charlatans will not mislead the people.

When the people live freely and fearlessly,
virtue will abound.

SUBMISSION

A well-governed state is like a woman.

Just as a woman, through cheerful and able service,
wins control over a man,
so a great state, by its peaceful generosity to smaller countries,
wins their allegiance;
and so a small state, by yielding to a great state,
wins influence over it.

Some submit to a conqueror,
others conquer by submitting.

Great states have no higher purpose
than to form a federation and feed the people.
Small states have no higher purpose
than to enter a federation and serve the people.

They have different ends;
but to achieve them,
both must practice submission.

THE SAVING TAO

The Tao is the sanctuary of all—
it is the good person's treasure,
and the bad person's last resort.

Beautiful words may sell goods,
but it takes kind actions to save people.

Why should people be put to death for their mistakes?
Even criminals can reform.

Better than riding a fine horse in the emperor's entourage,
is sitting and teaching the Tao to those who need it most.

The ancients esteemed the Tao
because those who seek it will find it,
and by it sinners can be saved.

Is it not so?
This is why the world honors the Tao.

SMALL BEGINNINGS

Avoid striving,
and practice non-doing.

Learn to taste the tasteless,
to grow the small things,
and to multiply the few.

Respond to hatred with kindness.
Resolve difficulties while they are easy,
and manage great things while they are small.

All the world's problems arise from slight causes,
and all great achievements have small beginnings.

The wise stay out of great affairs,
and so establish their greatness.
Many things that appear easy
are full of difficulties.

This is why the wise consider everything difficult—
so, in the end, they have no difficulties.

ATTEND TO THE END

That which is at rest is easily restrained;
that which has not yet appeared is easily prevented.
That which is weak is easily broken;
That which is meager is easily scattered.
Consider difficulties before they arise,
and order things before they become disorganized.

A mighty tree grows from a tiny seed.
A pagoda of nine stories is built from small bricks.
A journey of three thousand miles
begins with a single step.

Try to re-shape a thing, and you will deface it;
try to control it, and you will lose it.

The wise, accepting things as they are, deface nothing.
Not seizing things, they do not lose them.
While others, in their mad rush for wealth,
are always chasing success but coming up short.

To succeed, be as attentive at the end of an enterprise
as at the beginning.

The wise do not desire what they do not possess.
They learn to be unlearned;
they attend to that which others ignore.

In that spirit, they help things grow,
without interfering.

PROFOUND SIMPLICITY

In ancient times, rulers who followed the Tao
did not puff up the people,
but kept them simple-hearted.

Clever people are difficult to govern.
And so, governing people with cleverness is a mistake,
while governing with simplicity is a blessing to all.

Rulers who follow this become good models.
This is governing in the spirit of the Tao.

The effects of simplicity are profound indeed,
deep and far reaching.
It is the very opposite of common governing,
but it is the most effective way to rule.

LEAD FROM BELOW

Rivers and seas rule the land
by staying below it.

Wise rulers, desiring to lead the people,
humble themselves and stay below them;
wishing to help the people,
they stay out of the way.

Wise rulers live above
without burdening the people;
they guide without coercion.

They do not quarrel with anyone,
so no one quarrels with them.

This is why the world rejoices,
and never tires of a wise ruler.

COMPASSION

The Tao is by nature immaterial,
yet all the world calls it great.
It is because the Tao does not put on appearances
that it is great.

When a person puts on a show,
trying to appear great,
their mediocrity is soon exposed.

The Tao has three treasures
which the wise guard and cherish:
The first is compassion,
the second is economy,
the third is humility.

If you are compassionate, you can be truly courageous;
if you are economical, you can be truly generous;
if you are humble, you can be truly helpful.

If you are brave but lack compassion,
are generous but lack economy,
and try to help others but lack humility,
you've lost the way.

Compassion leads to victory in battle
and safety in defense.
Fortune blesses the compassionate.

BRING OUT THE BEST

The best warrior is not warlike;
the best fighter is not frenzied;
the best conqueror is not quarrelsome;
the best ruler is not unruly.

Bring out the best in yourself,
and you will bring out the best in others.

This is following the Tao.
Since ancient days, it is the way of virtue.

KNOW YOUR WEAKNESS

A great military general once said,
"I dare not invite conflict as a host,
but always act as a guest.
I hesitate to advance an inch,
and am quick to withdraw a foot."

This is advancing by not advancing;
it is winning without weapons;
it is charging without rage;
it is seizing without force.

There is no mistake greater
than making light of an enemy.
Through overconfidence,
we make ourselves vulnerable.

When well-matched armies come to conflict,
the one that is aware of its own weakness conquers.

HIDDEN TREASURE

My words are easy to understand,
and easy to put into practice—
yet no one in the world seems to understand them
or put them into practice.

Words have an ancestor—a preceding idea,
and deeds have a master—a preceding purpose.
As ideas and purposes are often misunderstood,
so I am misunderstood.

My words are precious beyond measure,
but I am not one to flaunt my riches.
The wise wear plain clothes
and keeps their gems out of sight.

NOT KNOWING

Not to know the things
you ought to know
is folly.

To know that there are some things
you cannot know
is wisdom.

The wise recognize the limits of their knowledge;
the foolish think they know everything.

ROOM TO BREATHE

When the people are too foolish to recognize danger,
disaster will surely come.

Do not confine the people in tight quarters
or they will chafe against your rule.
Give them room to breathe,
so they will not become restless.

The wise, while valuing themselves,
do not overestimate themselves.
They reject flattery and gain true merit.

COURAGE AND CAUTION

Reckless courage leads to death.
Cautious courage leads to life.
These two things, courage and caution,
must be balanced.

The right thing at one time
is the wrong thing at another.
This is why the wise approach everything
with both courage and caution.

The Tao does not fight, yet it conquers.
It makes no demands, yet it receives.
It issues no summons,
but things come to it naturally.

The Tao's reach is vast, indeed!
It casts a wide net, and loses nothing.

SHARP TOOLS

What good is it to threaten people with death?
If capital punishment was an effective deterrent,
no one would dare commit a crime.

When administering justice, be careful.
The executioner is like a skilled carpenter at his trade.
Do not try to take his place—
for if you pick up the carpenter's sharp tools,
you are liable to cut yourself.

OPPRESSION

When taxes are excessive,
the people starve.
When officials are overbearing,
the people rebel.
When governments make life miserable,
the people wish for death.

Oppressive measures never achieve
their intended results.

STAY FLEXIBLE

A living being is tender and flexible;
a corpse is hard and stiff.
It is the same with everything—
leaves and grasses are tender and delicate,
but when they die they become rigid and dry.

Those who are hard and inflexible
belong to death's domain;
but the gentle and flexible
belong to life.

As soon as a tree reaches its greatest height,
it begins to die.
The strongest soldiers are those
who refuse to conquer.

The strong stumble, and the mighty fall;
the tender and weak rise above.

THE USES OF WEALTH

The Tao resembles the stretching of a bow:
it humbles the mighty, and exalts the lowly;
it takes from those who have much
and gives to those in need.

This is the Tao—
it diminishes those who have abundance,
and lavishes those who lack.

The human way is just the opposite—
creditors take from those who lack
and give to those who already abound!

Where are the wealthy who will use
their riches to serve the world?

The wise earn much,
but claim it not for themselves.
They accomplish much,
but are not attached to their accomplishments.

They succeed abundantly,
yet make no show of their success.

PARADOXICAL TRUTHS

Nothing is gentler than water,
yet nothing can withstand its force.

Likewise, nothing compares to the Tao.
By it the weak defeat the strong;
and the flexible conquer the rigid.

Every one knows this is true,
but how few put it into practice!

Monks and priests are often the worst sinners.
Police officers and lawmakers
are often the worst criminals.

Truth is often paradoxical.

AVOID LAWSUITS

Wherever there is a legal dispute between two parties,
even after it is resolved,
bitterness remains.

How can this be avoided?

It is virtuous to keep one's obligations,
but the wise go beyond this—
they do not insist on their rights,
but forgive the debts of those who owe them.

They know that the Tao will reward them
for staying out of court.

HAPPY AT HOME

In a small country with few people,
government is still necessary—
but let it be very limited.

The people should be kept safe and content.
Then, though there are carriages and ships,
the people will not want to leave their country.

And though there are shields and swords,
there will be no reason to use them.

Then people will freely practice their trades,
delight in their cuisine,
be content with their clothes,
take pride in their homes,
and rejoice in their holidays.

Neighboring countries may be so near
that their dogs can be heard barking at night.
But your people will be so content,
they will grow old and die
without ever wanting to leave home!

TRUE WORDS

True words are often unpleasant;
pleasant words are often untrue.

Those who know the truth do not argue about it;
those who argue do not know the truth.

Scholars are seldom the wisest people;
the wise are seldom scholars.

Those who steal from others impoverish themselves;
those who give to others become rich.

Those who fight do not win;
those who win do not fight.

This is the way of the Tao.

A PREVIEW OF

THE MANUAL
A Philospher's Guide to Life

EPICTETUS

*Rendered by Sam Torode based on
a translation by Thomas Wentworth Higginson*

There are things that are within our power, and things that fall outside our power. Within our power are our own opinions, aims, desires, dislikes—in sum, our own thoughts and actions. Outside our power are our physical characteristics, the class into which we were born, our reputation in the eyes of others, and honors and offices that may be bestowed on us.

Working within our sphere of control, we are naturally free, independent, and strong. Beyond that sphere, we are weak, limited, and dependent. If you pin your hopes on things outside your control, taking upon yourself things which rightfully belong to others, you are liable to stumble, fall, suffer, and blame both gods and men. But if you focus your attention only on what is truly your own concern, and leave to others what concerns them, then you will be in charge of your interior life. No one will be able to harm or hinder you. You will blame no one, and have no enemies.

If you wish to have peace and contentment, release your attachment to all things outside your control. This is the path of freedom and happiness. If you want not just peace and contentment, but power and wealth too, you may forfeit the former in seeking the latter, and will lose your freedom and happiness along the way.

Whenever distress or displeasure arises in your mind, remind yourself, "This is only my interpretation, not reality itself." Then ask whether it falls within or outside your sphere of power. And, if it is beyond your power to control, let it go.

Desire demands the attainment of that which you desire, and aversion demands the avoidance of that which you dislike. Those who fail to attain their desires are disappointed. Those who attain what they dislike are distressed.

If you avoid only those undesirable things which are within your control, you will never suffer by attaining something you detest. But if you try to avoid what you cannot control—sickness, poverty, death—you will inflict useless mental suffering upon yourself.

End the habit of despising things that are not within your power, and apply your aversion to things that are within your power. As for desire, for now it is best to avoid it altogether. Those new to this philosophy must first secure their sphere of power, before they can discern what is worthy of desire. For if you desire things not within your power, you will suffer disappointment.

When practical necessity demands that you desire or avoid something external—at work, for instance—act with steady deliberation, not hasty strain.

What of things, objects, and beings that delight your mind, are of good practical use, or which you dearly love? Remind yourself of their true nature, beginning with the smallest trifle and working upward.

If you have a favorite cup, remember that it is only a cup that you prefer—if it is broken, you can bear it.

When you embrace your wife or child, remember that they are mortal beings. By accepting their nature rather than denying it, if either should die you will find the strength to bear it.

4

In preparing for any action, remind yourself of the nature of the action.

For instance, if you are going to a public pool, remind yourself of the usual incidents: people splashing, some pushing, some scolding, thieves stealing unguarded personal belongings. You will not be disturbed if you go into the experience prepared for such things and determined to retain inner harmony.

If something undesirable happens, you will be able to say, "My desire is not only to swim, but to remain in harmony with the nature of things. I cannot stay in harmony if I let myself become upset by things beyond my control."

And so it is with every act or experience.

People are not disturbed by things themselves, but by the views they take of those things. Even death is nothing to fear in itself, or Socrates would have run from it. The fear of death stems from the view that it is fearful.

When you are feeling upset, angry, or sad, don't blame another for your state of mind. Your condition is the result of your own opinions and interpretations.

People who are ignorant of philosophy blame others for their own misfortunes. Those who are beginning to learn philosophy blame themselves. Those who have mastered philosophy blame no one.

6

Do not take satisfaction in possessions and achievements that are not your own. If a horse were to say, "I am handsome," his pride may be excusable. But if you boast, "I have a handsome horse," you are claiming merit that is not yours.

What, then, is your own? The way you live your life.

When you are living in harmony with nature, you can take just satisfaction.

a preview of THE MANUAL

7

During a voyage, when the ship is anchored and you go ashore for supplies, you may amuse yourself with picking up some seashells and pretty stones along your way. But keep your thoughts tuned on the ship, remaining alert for the captain's call. You may need to drop your "treasures" and run back to the boat at any time.

Likewise in life, remain steadfast in pursuing your mission, always willing to shed distractions.

Do not wish that all things will go well with you, but that you will go well with all things.

9

Lameness may strike your leg, but not your resolve. Sickness may weaken your body, but not your determination—unless you let it. The only thing that can impede your will is your will itself.

Each time an obstacle arises, remind yourself of this truth. While it may hinder some part of you, it cannot constrain your true self.

Whenever a challenge arises, turn inward and ask what power you can exercise in the situation.

If you meet temptation, use self-control; if you meet pain, use fortitude; if you meet revulsion, use patience.

In this way, you will overcome life's challenges, rather than be overcome by them.

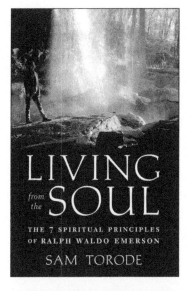
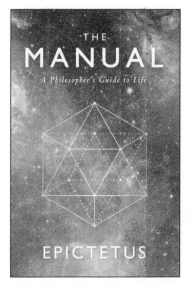
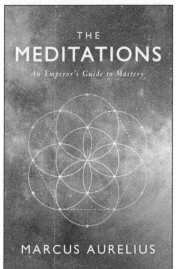